# The Ultimate Healthy Blender Cookbook

Fast and Easy Blender Recipes That are
Healthy and Tasty

BY

*Daniel Humphreys*

# License Notes

No part of this Book can be reproduced in any form or by any means including print, electronic, scanning or photocopying unless prior permission is granted by the author.

All ideas, suggestions and guidelines mentioned here are written for informative purposes. While the author has taken every possible step to ensure accuracy, all readers are advised to follow information at their own risk. The author cannot be held responsible for personal and/or commercial damages in case of misinterpreting and misunderstanding any part of this Book

# Table of Contents

# Introduction

Become a smoothie expert! Besides getting healthier each day by using the Ninja Blender to make delicious meal replacement smoothies, the nutritional tips in this book will make you more as aware of what you're eating and the nutritional benefits of each smoothie you whip up. You'll also become something of an expert once you start learning about all the vital and essential nutrients that your smoothie have in them.

So, get ready to enjoy some of the easiest, most delicious recipes you ever tasted—with just the push of a button—it's that simple. It's also fun—so why not get started now!

# Almond Milk

Making your own almond milk is simple and it taste delicious. Since your making your own you have complete control over how much sweetener, if any, to add. Remember, the nuts will need to be soaked for at least 4-6 hours before blending, so plan ahead by soaking them in water overnight. Almond milk is great for drinking, in your coffee, on your cereal, and for baking.

**Servings:** 5 cups

**Ingredients:**

- 1 1/2 cups raw almonds, blanched (can also use regular almonds)
- 4 cups water

**Optional additions:**

- 1 teaspoon vanilla extract
- 1/2 teaspoon cinnamon
- 1 tablespoon honey or other sweetener
- Pinch of sea salt

**Directions:**

Place almonds in a large bowl and cover with water. Soak for a minimum of 4 hours. The longer the better.

Strain off water and place almonds into your blender. Add 2 cups of water and blend for 2-3 minutes until a thick paste is formed.

Add in remaining water and any of the optional ingredients. Blend for another 2-3 minutes until milk is smooth and frothy.

Now it is time to strain the almond milk. Place a metal strainer over a large bowl. Spread a couple of layers of cheesecloth over the strainer. Slowly pour the almond milk through the strainer. Squeeze cheesecloth to remove excess milk.

Pour milk into glass container with cover and store in refrigerator for 3-4 days

# Coconut Milk

Coconut milk is very nutritious as it contains lauric acid and medium chain fatty acids which have been shown to be heart healthy and help with weight loss. It can be used in all kinds of recipes including smoothies, baked goods, curries, and as a standalone drink.

**Servings:** 4 cups

**Ingredients:**

- 2 cups shredded coconut, unsweetened
- 3 cups hot water

**Directions:**

Add coconut and water to blender. Process on high for 3-4 minutes or until desired consistency is reached.

To strain, place metal colander over large bowl. Line with a couple of layers of cheesecloth. Pour coconut milk through colander.

Store in glass container with cover in refrigerator for 3-4 days. Shake before serving.

# Sweet Vanilla Roasted Cashew Butter

Roasting the nuts before grinding enriches the flavor. This is a sweet and salty combination.

**Servings:** 1 cup

**Ingredients:**

- 3 cups cashews
- 3 tablespoons honey
- 1 teaspoon vanilla extract
- Pinch of sea salt
- ½ teaspoon cinnamon

**Directions:**

Heat oven to 350 degrees. Spread cashews on baking sheet in single layer (may need more than one pan).

Sprinkle cashews lightly with water. Place in oven and roast for 20 minutes, stirring once or twice during that time.

Remove nuts from oven and allow to cool.

Put cashews, honey, vanilla, salt, and cinnamon into blender. Start on low and then increase speed to high for 1 minute.

Check consistency and blend for up to 1 more minute.

Store in airtight container in refrigerator for up to 1 month.

# Sunflower Seed Butter

This very nutrition seed butter is a great alternative for people with nut allergens.

**Servings:** 1 ½ cups

**Ingredients:**

- 2 ½ cups raw sunflower seeds, hulled
- 2 tablespoons sunflower oil or coconut oil
- Pinch of sea salt

**Directions:**

Heat oven to 350 degrees F. Spread sunflower seeds in single layer on baking sheet(s). Roast for about 15 minutes or until golden brown, stirring frequently.

Remove from oven and allow to cool.

Put seeds, oil, and salt in blender. Start on low and then increase speed to high for 1 minute. Check consistency and blend for up to 1 more minute or until smooth and creamy.

Store in airtight container in refrigerator for up to 1 month.

# Black Bean Burgers

These high-protein burgers are packed with fiber and low in both calories and fat. Make a double batch to freeze for later.

**Servings:** 4

**Ingredients:**

- 1 (16 ounce) can black beans, drained and rinsed
- 1 medium yellow onion, diced
- 1 carrot, shredded
- 3 cloves garlic, minced
- ½ cup corn, fresh or frozen (thawed)
- 1 egg
- ½ cup Panko-style bread crumbs
- ¼ cup fresh cilantro, chopped
- 1 tablespoon cumin powder
- Salt and freshly ground black pepper, to taste

**Directions:**

Place all ingredients into blender. Pulse on and off, several times. Press ingredients down toward blades. Pulse a few more times.

Remove bean mixture from blender and place in bowl. Form into 4 patties.

Place patties onto lightly greased baking sheet. Bake in preheated 375 degree F oven for 10 minutes. Flip and bake another 10 minutes.

# Creamy Coconut-Pumpkin Soup

This creamy soup is perfect on a brisk autumn day.

**Servings:** 4

**Ingredients:**

- 2 cups chicken broth
- ½ cup coconut milk, unsweetened
- 1 (15 ounce) can pumpkin puree
- ½ onion, chopped
- 1 clove garlic, minced
- 1/2 teaspoon cayenne pepper
- ½ cup plain Greek yogurt
- 1 teaspoon honey
- Salt and freshly ground black pepper, to taste

**Directions:**

Place all ingredients into blender. Turn on low and slowly increase speed to high. Blend for 5-6 minutes until creamy.

Serve topped with croutons.

# Cream of Broccoli Soup

Cauliflower and almond milk give this soup its creamy texture.

**Servings:** 4

**Ingredients:**

- 1 tablespoon extra-virgin olive oil
- 1 medium yellow onion, chopped
- 3 garlic cloves, minced
- 1 small head cauliflower, chopped into florets
- 2 cups almond milk, unsweetened
- 2 cups chicken broth
- 3 cups broccoli florets, chopped
- Salt and freshly ground black pepper, to taste

**Directions:**

Heat olive oil in large saucepan over medium-high heat. Add onions and garlic and sauté for 2-3 minutes until onion turns translucent.

Add cauliflower, almond milk, chicken broth, and broccoli. Cover pot and bring to boil. Reduce heat and simmer, covered, for 10 minutes or until cauliflower and broccoli florets are soft.

Pour mixture into blender. Turn on low and slowly increase speed to high. Blend for 5-6 minutes until smooth.

Season with salt and pepper before serving.

# Tuscan White Bean Soup

This classic Italian soup is hearty enough to be a main course.

**Servings:** 6

**Ingredients:**

- 4 slices bacon, chopped
- 1 medium yellow onion, chopped
- 1 stalk celery, chopped
- 1 carrot, chopped
- 3 cloves garlic, minced
- 3 (16 ounce) cans cannellini beans, rinsed and drained
- 1 bay leaf
- 1/2 cup white wine
- 4 cups chicken broth
- 1/4 teaspoon crushed red pepper flakes
- 1/4 cup fresh basil
- Salt and freshly ground black pepper, to taste

**Directions:**

Heat saucepan over medium-high heat. Add bacon, onion, celery, carrot, and garlic. Cook, stirring occasionally, for 4-5 minutes. Add beans, bay leaf, wine, broth, red pepper flakes, and basil. Reduce heat, cover, and cook for 20 minutes, until vegetables are tender.

Add soup to blender. Turn blender on low and slowly increase speed to high. Blend for 30-40 seconds.

# Chimichurri Sauce

This sauce is of Argentinian origin and is popular on grilled meats.

**Servings:** Makes 1 1/2 cups

**Ingredients:**

- 1 1/2 cups fresh parsley
- 3 cloves garlic, crushed
- 3/4 cup extra virgin olive oil
- 3 tablespoons red wine vinegar
- 2 tablespoons dried oregano
- 2 teaspoons ground cumin
- 1/2 teaspoon salt
- 1/2 tablespoon hot sauce

**Directions:**

Place all ingredients in blender. Start on low and slowly increase speed to high. Blend for 30 seconds or until desired consistency is reached.

# Dark Chocolate Hazelnut Butter

This homemade version of Nutella is positively addicting.

**Servings:** 2 cups

## Ingredients:

- 2 ½ cups hazelnuts
- ¼ cup raw cacao nibs or 2 tablespoons cacao powder
- 3 tablespoons cane sugar or honey
- ½ teaspoon vanilla extract
- Pinch of sea salt

**Directions:**

Heat oven to 350 degrees F. Spread hazelnuts on baking sheet in single layer and roast in oven for 15 minutes, stirring once.

Remove hazelnuts from and oven place in clean dish towel while they are still hot. Fold towel around hazelnuts and massage with hands so nuts are rubbed against one another. This will cause skins to fall off.

Place hazelnuts in blender, discard skins.

Add cacao, sugar, vanilla, and salt to blender. Start on low and then increase speed to high for 1 minute. Check consistency and blend for up to 1 more minute or until consistency is creamy.

Store in airtight container in refrigerator for up to 1 month.

# Falafel

Okay, these aren't technically burgers, but they're pretty close. Serve these in pita bread topped with tahini sauce or on a platter with crudités and hummus.

**Servings:** 6

**Ingredients:**

- 2 (15.5 ounce) cans chickpeas, rinsed and drained
- 1 small onion, chopped
- 2-3 garlic cloves, chopped
- ½ cup parsley, chopped
- 1 teaspoon coriander
- 1 tablespoon cumin
- 1 teaspoon sea salt
- ½ teaspoon freshly ground black pepper
- 2 tablespoons whole wheat flour
- 1 tablespoon lemon juice
- 2-3 tablespoons olive oil

**Directions:**

Place all ingredients except for olive oil into blender. Set to variable 10 and pulse on and off until processed but still a little chunky.

Form mixture into golf-ball size balls. Chill in refrigerator for 30-60 minutes.

Heat olive oil in large frying pan over medium-high heat. Add balls in batches, and fry, turning, until all sides are golden brown, about 4-5 minutes. Set on paper-towel lined plate while cooking remaining batches.

# Curried Chickpea Burgers

These burgers are delicious when served in a whole-wheat pita and topped with tzatziki sauce.

**Servings:** 4

**Ingredients:**

- 1 small yellow onion, chopped
- 2 cloves garlic, chopped
- 1 carrot, shredded
- ¼ cup oats
- 3 eggs, lightly beaten
- 1 (15.5 ounce) can chickpeas, rinsed and drained
- ¼ cup Panko breadcrumbs
- 1 tablespoon lemon juice
- 2 teaspoons curry powder
- Salt and freshly ground black pepper, to taste
- 1 tablespoon olive oil

**Directions:**

Add onion, garlic, carrot, and oats to blender. Process on high for 30 seconds. Add remaining ingredients, except for olive oil, and pulse to mix, leaving mixture somewhat chunky. Form into 4 patties.

Heat 1 tablespoon olive oil in large skillet over medium-high heat. Add patties and cook until golden brown, about 5 minutes. Flip and cook on other side until golden brown, another 5 minutes.

Serve in warm pita pocket topped with tzatziki.

# Gazpacho

This garden-fresh soup is a cool treat on a summer day.

**Servings:** 4

**Ingredients:**

- 2 plum tomatoes, chopped
- ½ cucumber, chopped
- ½ green bell pepper, chopped
- ½ red bell pepper, chopped
- ½ red onion, chopped
- 1 clove garlic, minced
- 2 cups tomato juice
- ½ teaspoon dried oregano
- ½ teaspoon dried basil
- ½ teaspoon salt
- ¼ teaspoon black pepper
- 1 ½ teaspoons Worcestershire sauce
- 1 teaspoon lemon juice
- 2 teaspoons red wine vinegar

**Directions:**

Put tomatoes, cucumber, bell pepper, onion, and garlic into blender. Blend on high for about 30 seconds. Add remaining ingredients. Pulse a few times to mix.

Pour into container and chill in refrigerator for at least an hour before serving.

# Curried Parsnip and Pear Soup

The blending of parsnips and pears, with the spice of curry, makes for a unique and flavorful soup.

**Servings:** 4

**Ingredients:**

- 1 tablespoon olive oil
- 1 tablespoon butter
- 1 medium onion, chopped
- 1 tablespoon curry powder
- 1 teaspoon ground ginger
- 3 parsnips, peeled and sliced
- 2 large pears - peeled, cored, and chopped
- 4 cups chicken stock
- 1/2 cup coconut milk
- Salt and freshly ground black pepper, to taste
- 1 pear, sliced, for garnish
- Yogurt for serving (optional)

**Directions:**

Heat olive oil and butter in a saucepan over medium heat. Add onion, ginger, and curry powder, and then sauté until onion softens, about 5 minutes.

Add parsnips and pears and stir to coat. Add chicken stock, bring to boil, reduce heat and simmer for 15-20 minutes until parsnips are soft.

Pour mixture into blender. Add coconut milk, salt, and pepper. Turn blender on low and slowly increase speed to high. Blend for 30-40 seconds.

Serve garnished with slice of pear and spoonful of yogurt.

# Red Pepper Hummus

Change up your traditional hummus with this red pepper variation.

**Servings:** 8

**Ingredients:**

- 1 (16 ounce) can chick peas, drained and rinsed
- 1 tablespoon extra-virgin olive oil
- 1 medium red bell pepper, chopped
- 2 cloves garlic, crushed
- 1 tablespoon tahini
- Juice of 1 lemon
- 1 teaspoon ground cumin
- 1/2 teaspoon cayenne pepper
- 1/4 cup fresh basil
- 1/2 teaspoon salt
- 1/4 teaspoon ground black pepper

**Directions:**

Place all ingredients in blender. Start on low and slowly increase speed to high. Blend for 1 minute or until desired consistency is reached.

# Tzatziki

This traditional Greek dip gets better as it sits so make it the day before if you can.

**Servings:** 5 cups

**Ingredients:**

- 1 (32 ounce) container plain Greek style yogurt
- 1 English cucumber with peel, diced, divided in half
- 1 clove garlic, pressed
- 2 tablespoons fresh lime juice
- 2 tablespoons extra-virgin olive oil
- 2 teaspoons grated lemon zest
- 3 tablespoons chopped fresh dill
- 1 teaspoon salt

**Directions:**

Place yogurt, 1/2 of cucumber, garlic, lemon juice, olive oil, lemon zest, dill, salt, and pepper in blender. Pulse on and off, several times. Should still be a little chunky. Check consistency and pulse a few more times if needed.

Pour into serving dish, top with remaining chopped cucumber, cover and refrigerate for at least a couple of hours and preferably overnight.

# Black Bean Hummus

Quick and easy, this tastes great as a sandwich with thick-cut tomatoes and crisp romaine lettuce.

**Servings:** 1 1/2 cups

**Ingredients:**

- 1 (15 ounce) can black beans, rinsed and drained
- 2 cloves garlic, crushed
- 2 teaspoons lemon juice
- 1 tablespoon dried basil
- 1 teaspoon sesame oil
- 1/4 teaspoon cayenne pepper
- 1/4 teaspoon paprika

**Directions:**

Place all ingredients in blender. Start on low and slowly increase speed to high. Blend for 1-2 minutes or until desired consistency has been reached.

# Lemon-Dill Yogurt Dressing

A tangy dip, try it in place of mayonnaise on potato salad.

**Servings:** Makes 1 cup

**Ingredients:**

- 1 cup plain Greek yogurt
- 1 tablespoon fresh lemon juice
- 1 teaspoon grated lemon zest
- 1/4 cup extra-virgin olive oil
- 1/4 teaspoon ground black pepper
- 2 teaspoons fresh dill, chopped

**Directions:**

Put all the ingredients in blender. Start on low and slowly increase speed to high. Blend for 30 seconds until a desired consistency is reached.

Chill in refrigerator for at least an hour before serving.

# Black Bean and Beet Burgers

Another take on black bean burgers, this time with the antioxidant power of beets.

**Servings:** 4

**Ingredients:**

- 1 (16 ounce) can black beans
- 2 medium beets, cooked, cut into chunks
- ½ red onion, chopped
- ½ cup brown rice, cooked
- 2 cloves garlic, minced
- 1 teaspoon paprika
- 1 teaspoon cumin
- Salt and freshly ground black pepper, to taste

**Directions:**

Preheat oven to 400 degrees F.

Place all ingredients into blender. Pulse on and off, several times. Press ingredients down toward blades. Pulse a few more times.

Remove mixture from blender and place in bowl. Taste and adjust seasonings as needed. Form into 4 patties.

Place patties onto lightly greased baking sheet (or use parchment paper). Bake in preheated 400 degree F oven for 15 minutes. Flip and bake another 10 minutes, until burgers are lightly browned and crisp.

# Walnut-Rice Burgers

These burgers can be frozen after cooking and microwaved for a quick and healthy meal.

**Servings:** 8

**Ingredients:**

- 2 cups brown rice, cooked
- 1 cup walnuts
- 2 tablespoons olive oil, divided
- ½ small yellow onion, diced
- 2 cloves garlic, minced
- 1 stalk celery, chopped
- 1 small carrot, chopped
- ½ teaspoon cayenne pepper
- ½ teaspoon dried ginger powder
- 1 teaspoon dried basil
- 1 teaspoon dried thyme
- ¼ cup fresh parsley
- ¼ cup whole wheat flour
- 1 egg, beaten
- Salt and freshly ground black pepper, to taste

**Directions:**

Heat 1 tablespoon olive oil in large skillet over medium-high heat. Add onion, garlic, celery, and carrots and sauté for 5-6 minutes until vegetables soften.

Add rice, walnuts, vegetables, seasonings, parsley, flour, egg, salt, and pepper to blender.

Blend on high for about a minute. Press ingredients down toward blades. Pulse a few more times.

Remove mixture from blender and form into 8 patties.

Heat 1 tablespoon olive oil in large skillet over medium-high heat. Add patties and cook until lightly browned, about 5 minutes. Flip and cook on other side until lightly browned, another 5 minutes.

# Peanut Butter

Making your own peanut butter ensures that it doesn't have trans fats or huge amounts of added sugar.

**Servings:** 1 cup

**Ingredients:**

- 3 cups raw peanuts
- ½ cup oil – olive oil, sunflower oil, or peanut oil are all acceptable

**Directions:**

Pinch of sea salt

Put peanuts, oil and salt into blender. Start on low and then bring it up to high speed. Blend for 60 seconds. Check consistency. Blend for another 30-60 seconds if needed.

Store in airtight container in refrigerator for up to 3-4 weeks.

# Chocolate Almond Milk

Rich dark chocolate and nutty taste is like a candy bar in a glass.

**Servings:** 4

**Ingredients:**

- 1 cup raw almonds, blanched
- 4 cups water
- 1/4 cup raw cacao nibs
- Pinch of salt
- 1 tablespoon honey or maple syrup (optional)

**Directions:**

Place almonds in a large bowl and cover with water. Soak for a minimum of 4 hours and preferable overnight.

Strain off water and place almonds into your blender. Add 2 cups of water and blend for 2-3 minutes until a thick paste is formed.

Add in remaining water, cacao nibs, salt, and honey or maple syrup. Blend for another 2-3 minutes until milk is smooth and frothy.

Place a metal strainer over a large bowl. Spread a couple of layers of cheesecloth over the strainer. Slowly pour the almond milk through the strainer. Squeeze cheesecloth to remove excess milk.

Pour milk into glass container with cover and store in refrigerator for 3-4 days.

# Almond Butter

Almond butter is becoming increasingly popular as an alternative to peanut butter. Almond butter is rich in vitamin E, potassium, magnesium, iron, calcium, phosphorus, fiber, and healthy monounsaturated fats. Plus, you can make your own at a fraction of the cost of store bought.

**Servings:** 1 cup

**Ingredients:**

- 3 cups almonds, raw or roasted
- ½ cup oil (optional, adding oil will give a creamier butter)

**Directions:**

Place nuts in blender. Add oil if desired. Turn blender to low and then increase to high. Blend for 1 minute. Check consistency, blend for additional minute if needed.

Store in airtight container in refrigerator for up to 1 month.

# Macadamia-Cashew Nut Butter

Rich, creamy, delicious, this combination is so good you will want to eat it by the spoonful.

**Servings:** 2 cups

**Ingredients:**

- 2 cups macadamia nuts
- 1 cup cashews
- 2 tablespoon coconut oil
- 3-4 tablespoons pure maple syrup
- 1 teaspoon vanilla extract
- Pinch of salt (generous)

**Directions:**

Add macadamia nuts and cashews to blender. Process for about a minute. Add coconut oil, maple syrup, vanilla, and salt. Blend for an additional minute or until desired creaminess is reached.

Store in airtight container in refrigerator for up to a month.

# Ketchup

Store bought ketchup is loaded with sugar, dyes, and fillers. Make your own for a health and flavor boost.

**Servings:** Makes 4 cups

**Ingredients:**

- 28-oz. can tomato puree
- 1 medium yellow onion, peeled and quartered
- 2 cloves garlic, crushed
- 2 tablespoons brown sugar
- 1/2 cup cider vinegar
- 1 cup water
- 1 teaspoon dry mustard
- ½ teaspoon cayenne pepper
- ½ teaspoon ground allspice
- ½ teaspoon ground ginger
- ½ teaspoon ground cinnamon
- ½ teaspoon sea salt
- ½ teaspoon ground black pepper

**Directions:**

Add all ingredients to blender. Blend on high for 30 seconds or until smooth.

Pour into large saucepan, bring to boil, reduce heat, and simmer for an hour, stirring occasionally.

Pour into airtight containers and store in refrigerator for up to a month.

# Homemade Applesauce

This is simple and much better than jarred applesauce.

**Servings:** 4

**Ingredients:**

- 4 apples, peeled, cored, chopped
- ¾ cup water
- 1/2 teaspoon cinnamon
- ¼ cup brown sugar

**Directions:**

Place apples into saucepan and add about an inch of water. Bring to boil, reduce heat, cover and simmer for about 5 minutes or until apples are tender.

Add apples along with remaining ingredients to blender. Blend, starting on low and then increasing to high for about 30 seconds or until desired consistency.

# African Sweet Potato and Peanut Soup

This flavorful soup combines the tastes of sweet potatoes, peanuts, cilantro, and tomatoes into a fabulous combination.

**Servings:** 6

**Ingredients:**

- 1 tablespoon olive oil
- 1 large yellow onion, chopped
- 3 cloves garlic, minced
- 2 teaspoons fresh ginger, minced
- 1 ½ teaspoons ground cumin
- 1 ½ teaspoons ground coriander
- ½ teaspoon cinnamon
- ¼ teaspoon ground cloves
- 1 (16 ounce) can chopped tomatoes
- 3 large sweet potatoes, peeled and cubed
- 1 large carrot, sliced
- 4 cups chicken broth
- ¼ teaspoon cayenne pepper
- 2 tablespoons peanut butter
- ¼ cup roasted peanuts, unsalted, chopped
- 1 bunch fresh cilantro chopped

**Directions:**

In a large saucepan, heat olive oil over medium-high heat. Add onion and sauté for 5-6 minutes until soft. Add garlic, cumin, coriander, cinnamon, and cloves. Sauté for another minute. Add tomatoes, sweet potatoes, carrot, and chicken broth. Bring to boil, reduce heat and simmer, covered for 30 minutes.

Pour soup into blender. Add cayenne pepper and peanut butter. Turn blender on low and slowly increase speed to high. Blend for 30-40 seconds.

Serve topped chopped peanuts and cilantro.

# Coconut Butter

Making your own coconut butter couldn't be simpler and will definitely save you money. Coconut butter has a rich coconut taste and is extremely versatile. It can be used in baking, added to smoothies, or stirred into your morning coffee in place of cream for a rich nutty taste.

**Servings:** 2 ½ cups

**Ingredients:**

- 6 cups coconut flakes, unsweetened

**Directions:**

Pour coconut flakes into blender. Blend on high for 60 seconds. Push down a coconut flakes from side of blender. Process for another minute or until desired consistency is reached.

Coconut butter can be stored at room temperature in an airtight container for several months. If stored in refrigerator butter will turn hard—bring to room temperature to soften.

# Spicy Chicken Burgers

Making your own chicken burgers is very easy with the help of your Ninja Blender.

**Servings:** 4

**Ingredients:**

- 1 pound boneless, skinless chicken, cut into chunks
- 1 medium white onion, diced
- 1 medium red bell pepper, diced
- 2 cloves garlic
- 1 tablespoon Dijon mustard
- ½ cup bread crumbs
- ¼ cup fresh cilantro
- 2 tablespoons lime juice
- 1 tablespoon hot sauce
- 1 teaspoon chili powder
- 1 teaspoon cumin
- Salt and freshly ground black pepper, to taste

**Directions:**

Place all ingredients into blender. Pulse on and off several times. Press ingredients down toward blades. Pulse a few more times.

Remove mixture from blender and form into 4 patties.

Cook patties on grill or frying pan until no longer pink in center, about 4-5 minutes per side.

# Chickpea, Sesame, And Carrot Burger

Another take on the ever-popular chickpea burgers. Try these on the grill at your next barbecue.

**Servings:** 6

**Ingredients:**

- 1 (15.5 ounce) can chickpeas
- 1 cup shredded carrots, divided
- 1 small yellow onion, diced
- 2 tablespoons tahini paste
- 1 teaspoon cumin
- 1 egg, lightly beaten
- 3 tablespoons olive oil, divided
- ½ cup breadcrumbs
- 1 teaspoon lemon juice
- 3 tablespoons sesame seeds
- Salt and freshly ground black pepper, to taste

**Directions:**

Put chickpeas, ½ cup carrots, onion, tahini, cumin, and egg into blender. Blend on high for about 1 minute until paste-like consistency is reached. Scoop mixture into bowl.

Heat 1 tablespoon olive oil in large skillet over medium-high heat. Add remaining ½ cup of carrots and cook until softened, about 5-6 minutes.

Add cooked carrots, breadcrumbs, lemon juice, sesame seeds, salt, and pepper to bowl with chickpea mixture.

Mix together using hands or wooden spoon.

Form mixture into 6 equal-size patties. Brush each side with olive oil and cook on preheated grill until golden brown, about 5 minutes per side. Alternatively, cook in skillet over medium-high heat.

# Creamy Potato-Leek Soup

This is a thick, creamy soup. Serve with crusty bread for a complete meal.

**Servings:** 4

**Ingredients:**

- 6 medium potatoes, peeled and cubed
- 1 tablespoon olive oil
- 2 leeks, washed, chopped
- 2 stalks celery, chopped
- 2 cup chicken broth
- 1 ½ cups heavy cream
- 1 teaspoon dried thyme
- Sea salt and freshly ground black pepper, to taste

**Directions:**

Place potatoes in large pot, cover with water, bring to boil, reduce heat and simmer for 20 minutes or until potatoes are tender.

In a medium skillet, heat olive oil over medium-high heat. Add leeks and celery and sauté for 7-8 minutes or until leeks are tender.

Add potatoes, leek mixture, chicken broth, heavy creamy, thyme, salt, and pepper to blender. Turn blender on low and slowly increase speed to high. Blend for 30-40 seconds.

Serve garnished with croutons.

# Author's Afterthoughts

*Thanks ever so much to each of my cherished readers for investing the time to read this book!*

*I know you could have picked from many other books but you chose this one. So a big thanks for downloading this book and reading all the way to the end.*

*If you enjoyed this book or received value from it, I'd like to ask you for a favor. Please take a few minutes to post an honest and heartfelt review on Amazon.com. Your support does make a difference and helps to benefit other people.*

*Thanks!*

**Daniel Humphreys**

# About the Author

***Daniel Humphreys***

Many people will ask me if I am German or Norman, and my answer is that I am 100% unique! Joking aside, I owe my cooking influence mainly to my mother who was British! I can certainly make a mean Sheppard's pie, but when it comes to preparing Bratwurst sausages and drinking beer with friends, I am also all in!

I am taking you on this culinary journey with me and hope you can appreciate my diversified background. In my 15 years career as a chef, I never had a dish returned to me by one of clients, so that should say something about me! Actually, I will take that back. My worst critic is my four years old son, who refuses to taste anything that is green color. That shall pass, I am sure.

My hope is to help my children discover the joy of cooking and sharing their creations with their loved ones, like I did all my life. When you develop a passion for cooking and my suspicious is that you have one as well, it usually sticks for life. The best advice I can give anyone as a professional chef is invest. Invest your time, your heart in each meal you are creating. Invest also a little money in good cooking hardware and quality ingredients. But most of all enjoy every meal you prepare with YOUR friends and family!

Made in the USA
Las Vegas, NV
17 December 2023

83044295R00049